I'm glad you didn't die Mummy

Tracey Okines

Working as a model, aged 21

I'm glad you didn't die Mummy

by Tracey Okines

First published by Amazon in 2020

Tracey Okines is identified as the author of this book in accordance with Section 77 of the Copyright, Designs and Patent Act, 1988

Tracey Okines © 2020

Thanks to everyone who has helped me with this book

Prologue

This is a true story. I was a young working mum. Now I have Locked-in Syndrome. This book is about how it changed my life. Other people typed it up for me. I spelt out what I wanted to say using my eyes and a letter board. My parents have written, at the end of the book, about how they felt at this time.

Contents

Chapter 1

Life changed forever

I never thought I would end up like this. I thought about loss of a limb, death of a loved one, even death, but I never imagined that I would end up disabled. Some people describe Locked-in Syndrome as being buried alive or being trapped in their own body. For me it is like being in limbo land. I am not dead and not quite alive.

I awoke in a dark room. The only light was the sun searing through what appeared to be a large square door with a rectangular window to the left of it. I could hear the rustling of the leaves on the trees and the purring from car engines. I guessed I was in hospital by the nee-naw sound of ambulances going past my window. I closed my eyes and everything went black again.

I was told what had happened to me but I didn't take the information in for months as I was doped up on medical drugs. People said it must have been strange going to sleep in my nice double-bed at home and waking up in a single bed in hospital. But no, I felt nothing.

I'd gone to a gymnastics club at my gym on the Thursday evening with my boyfriend at the time, my daughter, my boyfriend's uncle and his daughters. We had been asked to cartwheel to the other end of the mat. Being cocky and showing off I did my cartwheels with no hands. I had successfully completed these before but this time I landed on my head. Unbeknown to me I burst a blood clot which was from a main artery in my neck. I don't remember gaining my injury. I remember my right leg really hurt and my right ankle swelled up. I couldn't put pressure on my leg. I hopped over to the lady who ran the gymnastics club telling her what I had done. She ushered me away and told me it was my own fault for being silly. I limped my way through the next few activities then I went home and immersed my foot in cold water trying to reduce the swelling.

I went to work the next day and explained to my friend Jane what had happened. She laughed and said I was the only person she knew who felt worse coming out of the gym than going into the gym! I laughed. If my ankle was not better by Monday, I said, I would go to see my doctor. I finished my shift.

I loved my job as a nursery nurse. I worked with the two to three-year-olds. I loved their little faces as they achieved something new. I was the lively, active person at work. I loved dancing and could not really sit still. The job really suited me. I was told that I brought energy to the setting.

I rushed home, pulled on a pair of oversized green wellies and took my puppy to the woods. My puppy was about eight months old and was a Jack Russell crossed with a Staffordshire Bull Terrier, crossed with a German Shepherd. I looked up at the trees above me and held out my arms as though embracing the sky. I could hear my puppy crunching on fallen leaves behind me and the pitter-patter of light rain on the leaves above my head. At that moment I felt very lucky. I had a beautiful and clever six-year old daughter. I had a funny little puppy. I had just handed in the notice on my flat to get a two double-bedroom garden flat.

I loved my life. I did moan sometimes about being a single mum, but I wouldn't have swopped my daughter or my life for the world. I finished walking my dog and throwing him sticks, then I rushed home for a cup of tea.

That evening I went to a party at my friend's. The girls from work were there. We did not need alcohol to get us going. I went outside for a cigarette and when I came back inside, I felt awful. I felt dizzy and light-headed. I had to sit down before I fell down. I didn't normally suffer from headaches but my head was pounding. My friend gave me some co-codamol. I felt better but I could not shift my headache.

After the party I was meant to go clubbing with some of the girls. I was known as the life and soul of the party but I decided to go home at the end of the party. One of my friends gave me a lift.

I limped up the stairs to my flat and was met by the open arms of my boyfriend. As tears rolled down my cheeks, I complained that my head was hurting. My boyfriend suggested that I went to bed. I thought it was a good idea to sleep it off. I can't remember going to bed that night. I must have gone to sleep as soon as my head hit the pillow. Apparently, as I slept, I had a fit. I'd never had a fit before. My boyfriend didn't ring an ambulance as I had gone back to normal.

I cannot remember the weekend that followed, the last weekend of January 2008. I usually went to my parents' house on Saturdays but that Saturday my Dad told me that I had sent him a text saying that the weather was nice so I would take my daughter out instead. Earlier that day I was sitting in my lounge. I remember holding up my right hand and twisting it around wondering how it worked. There are blanks in my memory. I can't remember Sunday. On the Monday I remember sitting at a friend's house and eating a ham salad roll which I'd purchased from a bakery. I was told that I'd gone to my doctor's complaining of severe head pain. I was sent away with headache tablets. I cannot remember picking my daughter up from school that day but I remember dropping her off at a friend's house later. My friend lives opposite my flat. She has a daughter who is a year younger than mine.

That evening I went salsa dancing with my boyfriend, Justin, and his uncle. I enjoyed the salsa dancing and remember limping as I did the moves because my ankle still hurt following the fall. When the class was over, I went upstairs to the bar and had a drink. I don't remember going home that evening but I remember putting my daughter to bed. I remember going to my front room where Justin and his uncle were sitting. Apparently I vomited. I only remember that my head hurt and I felt really light-headed. I can't remember but I must have gone to bed. I started fitting. Justin put me in the recovery position a few times. Needless to say I just fitted out of it. Justin phoned for an ambulance. The paramedic said that if they had got to me sooner my injuries wouldn't have been so extensive. I was taken to hospital and stabilised.

Chapter 2

Coming out of a coma

My parents got a call from the hospital at three o'clock in the morning and were told to expect the worst. I stayed in a coma for about a month. I had dreams in the coma. They are as vivid to me now as though I had seen them yesterday. In the dreams I was racing along on solid snow. I was sitting on a seat opposite an unknown man. I was sitting in a semi-circle that was attached to what looked like a motorbike like those on Star Wars. One of my ex's drove along in his truck and got out. He pointed at me and said, "That one is still alive!" On further investigation the driver of the motorbike realised my ex was right. He rushed me to the hospital.

At the hospital I could see nurses running around in front of me. One kept repeating my name. I could see what looked like different coloured aliens from the film 'Mars Attacks'. They had formed a line in my field of vision and as each coloured alien walked past my sight, they jumped head-first exploding into a splatpuddle. All I could hear was my voice inside my head saying, "When you see the green aliens, you are dead". But I never saw a green alien!

Next I was walking down a snowy hill. There were no footprints being left behind me. At the bottom of the hill was a hospital. It had a roof made of blue tarpaulin that was held up by long wooden sticks. Someone was shoving a pencil into my hand. I couldn't write my name. I was attempting to move my hand but it wouldn't move. I could hear what sounded like two beats of a glockenspiel being played backwards like a dong-ding instead of a ding-dong. I was lying in the snow face down. I could hear the beats. As they faded I found myself in the room of a hospital. I looked down at my name badge to see that I was a neurosurgeon. I had never even used that word before.

I kept dreaming and dreaming then one day I just woke up. I wasn't sure what had happened. It later became clear to me. Following my fit I had a stroke and fell into a coma. The surgeon told my parents that I probably wouldn't survive the coma or, if I did pull through, I would be a vegetable. I wondered what vegetable I would be? Maybe a carrot? I look a bit like a carrot! I'm long and skinny anyway.

I was 27 years old and had had a stroke. I thought only old people had strokes. How wrong was I? In my coma I'd had a blood transfusion because so much blood had been taken from me and it had to be replaced. The part of my brain which sends signals to my muscles was starved of oxygen so it had died. I had a tube going up my nose and into my stomach. This was how food was fed to me. I remember the tube made my throat sore. For days no-one knew how I had sustained my injury. Using keyhole surgery a camera was inserted into a vein in my leg. It went up my body but it stopped at my neck. Surgeons realised I had a blood clot in my neck.

This was when I got treated for what was actually wrong. I had a tracheostomy which allowed me to breathe easier. I stayed in my coma for four weeks. During this time I must have been on some strong drugs because I had some very weird dreams. I woke up in a dark room. I could see nurses as they came to check on me. I thought I was in a computer game and I had to hide. If I closed my eyes, I could not see anyone and in my mind, I thought no-one could see me.

I think it is a good idea to talk to a person who is in a coma. They may not be able to make out what you are saying but when people spoke to me, I envisioned them in my dreams. That is how I know who visited me. When my parents were clearing out my flat I remembered dreaming about them explaining to me about my possessions. When my dog went to my friend, I dreamt about my mother sneezing in my dog's presence because animal fur makes her sneeze. When my coil was removed, I dreamt that I was removing a very large tampon.

Waking up from a coma is unlike waking up from sleep. It took me months to realise what was going on. I wasn't scared, in fact I was very calm. I knew I was in hospital for a reason. I knew nothing about Locked-in Syndrome. My parents researched the condition on the internet. We found out that the condition is quite rare, which is good. I wouldn't wish this on my worst enemy.

Before I realised that I was paralysed I just thought that I was being good and not moving and making myself better. I didn't realise that I couldn't move if I tried. A lot of people have different views on being paralysed. To me it feels as though there are weights tied to every one of my muscles, stopping me from moving. I know what I should do to make my muscles work and I can feel myself moving, but when I look down I am as still as a statue. Being paralysed means that I can't do anything for myself.

I first realised this in hospital. They were giving me laxatives to regulate my bowels as I had no control of my movements at all. I woke up to find a load of strangers and my father cleaning my rear end. I was mortified. Being paralysed meant that I couldn't move any of my muscles so I couldn't eat, drink or speak. Don't worry, I didn't starve. After a while they took out the tube that went up my nose and I was fed through what is called a PEG tube. The tube went through a hole which was made in my skin and it allowed food, drink and medication to go straight into my stomach. I couldn't feel anything going into my stomach unless it was very hot or cold. If I regurgitated, I could taste my food.

People ask me if I miss food? My answer is no, not really. Sometimes I really fancy a fry up or something but I love the smell of food. I am sure I will eat again.

With my parents

Chapter 3

Being heard

I couldn't have people deciding things for me anymore. I found it very difficult to look from left to right so my parents encouraged me just to move my eyes up and down to say "yes" and "no". I was able to communicate with others but only if they asked me the correct question. For example, I could answer "Are you too hot?", "Are you in pain?" or "Did you have a nice day?". It opened up a new world of possibilities for me.

People still came into my room and just presumed that I couldn't think. If people talked to me, I felt privileged. People spoke to me slowly and loudly. In my head I was screaming, "I am not deaf". I have some advice for anyone who cannot speak: have a signal for "I don't know". There are many times when I have been asked a question and I've been called a liar because I just don't know the answer. I just answered 'Yes' or 'No' because sometimes it's easier to get people to back off.

I used to be a chatterbox, I used to talk a lot. Since my accident I've learnt to listen. With my ability to remember things, I have learnt a lot about people. I am good at reading body language which helps me understand others.

Yes, I admit it, I have taken drugs before but they definitely weren't the cause of my accident. I am only saying this because when I was first admitted to hospital, I tested positive for having traces of some substance in my system. Taking drugs is not something I would recommend to others but it is something that I did and I can't change back the hands of time. When I was admitted a lot of people, including medical staff, just presumed that I had taken a drug overdose. I hadn't made matters any easier by testing positive in the first place. It wasn't like I took them all the time. Sometimes I went months, even years, without taking anything. If I didn't have anything it didn't bother me.

So I woke up in hospital and that was where I stayed for five and a half months. I don't remember clearly all of those five and a half months. I remember what some of the people looked like but I can't remember all their names. I was very ill and my memories are a bit blurry. I had a chest infection, pneumonia, thrush in the throat, a urine infection and to top all that off I had MRSA. I didn't realise I was so ill. I just did what I was told to do like a robot.

There were no shower or bath facilities at the hospital unless you were in the spinal injuries unit so I had to have bed baths for five and a half months. I felt like I was smelly. Whether I did smell or not I will never know. I remember looking at the ceiling and wondering how my daughter was. I wondered what she was doing and I kept thinking that I had to collect her from school. As the afternoon approached and the time came to collect her went past, I got more and more angry at myself for not getting up. I kept thinking "I will try harder tomorrow".

I couldn't feel my body change. I was on too many painkillers to feel anything. I have a new-found respect for disabled people. I just presumed that people were disabled from birth and wondered why they moaned if that is all they've ever known. Now I admire disabled people, young and old.

I remember the fog in my mind fading and reality began to hit. Before my accident I took everything for granted, especially my health. I thought this would never happen to me. This sort of thing happens to other people. I never imagined that I would experience this in my lifetime. There was nothing to do so I learnt about all aspects of my condition and about nursing. I could easily complete a nursing examination. I have learnt some medical jargon and procedures that I didn't know existed at the beginning. I was suctioned over 30 times a day. Suctioning is where a thin, long tube is put directly into the lungs via the tracheostomy or mouth. The tube tickles the lungs, producing a cough, loosening the secretions and allowing them to be sucked up through a tube. A lot of people cannot cough after a stroke. I have a very strong cough and I cough when I need to. My cough jerks me about. Believe me, it looks a lot worse than it is.

With my friend Sarah

Chapter 4

A new life dawns

I was in the high dependency unit. My consultant did not want me on the ward as I could not call out or defend myself if I got attacked. I remember people coming into my room with aprons and examination gloves on and some people wore full-face visors. I got poked, prodded and examined by every professional I thought was possible. I knew it was for my own good so I let it happen. I got used to having needles put in me.

After a few months I began to see the world more clearly and reality hit hard. I realised that the world I had once loved had gone. The daughter I had once lived with went to live with my sister and nephew. I didn't get on very well with my sister but I knew that my daughter would be well looked after. My dog was re-homed to a friend of mine so I knew that he would be safe and happy. Of course, my work couldn't keep my job open for me so someone else got the vacancy. I had already handed in the notice on my flat and my parents were being told by surgeons that I probably wouldn't survive. My possessions were bagged up and taken to the tip. Most of my clothes didn't fit any more and they definitely weren't suitable. Most of them had no stretch in them so I couldn't get them on. To top everything, hardly any of my so-called friends came to see me. I never saw Justin again.

Justin and I first met when we were both doing an art course. We were only about 18 years old and we were both dating other people. We bumped into each other again in the years following college. Finally, we were both single. One thing led to another and before long we were a couple. He was really funny and was good with my daughter. We got on well. But I thought we had the same ideas about love.

At the time of my accident I had only been with Justin for about four months although I'd known him for about nine years. I knew he was not responsible for my fit and I was glad that he had finally phoned for an ambulance so that my daughter hadn't seen me fitting. The paramedics at the scene had said that if they had got to me earlier then the extent of my injuries would not be so vast. I still hated him for about a year and I didn't expect him to stay around but a note to say goodbye would have been nice. I thought that if you cared for someone then you did what you could to protect them. However, I stopped focussing on what could have been and concentrated on what did happen.

I learnt all about tracheostomies. Before my accident I had never even heard of a tracheostomy, which is an opening in the front of the neck so that a tube can be inserted into the windpipe to help you breath. I now know how to change one and how to change an inner tube. I know the difference between a normal and a filtrated inner tube, a speaking valve and capping. I learnt about bedpans. It is difficult to go to the toilet when you are lying down. I learnt about splints and chest physio. This journey has been a learning curve for me. This is a road which I never chose to take but a road which I was plonked on instead.

Chapter 5

Using a communication board

I went to sleep and when I woke up my entire life was different and there was nothing I could do to change things. I just had to make the best of a bad situation. I was so fed up with just answering 'Yes' or 'No' questions. I was unable to express myself or say what I wanted to say. It was very frustrating. My Dad bought me different communication boards to try but I was unsuccessful with them. Then my Dad found a board on a French Locked-in Syndrome website. It had five different colours: red, yellow, blue, green and orange. Each colour contains letters and each line of colours starts with a vowel. For example, Red will contain A, B, C and D and Yellow will contain E, F, G and H. The person I am communicating with will read each colour in the order Red, Yellow, Blue, Green, Orange. I look up when the person gets to the correct colour and the person then reels off the letters in that colour, so for yellow it will be E, F, G and H. I look up when the person gets to the correct letter. The person will then write a letter down until a word is formed, then a sentence can be formed.

At first, communicating in this way was very slow and tedious but as I got more used to the board I got quicker. It is still slow but it is better than nothing. Most days I am OK with the speed at which I can communicate but I get so frustrated. I am used to saying what I want when I want. It has been a long time since I last communicated verbally so I forget that people may not be able to understand me because they give me a look of confusion.

People ask me if I am OK. I answer with my eyes and I look up. Sometimes I realise that the person doesn't understand me and thinks I am ignoring them or that I don't understand them. I have started nodding for 'Yes' and shaking my head for 'No' so people may find it easier to understand me. Over time I have learnt to say only what is absolutely necessary. Because people write down what I am saying I cannot express myself or use different vocal tones. Sometimes, because a conversation moves fast and it takes me so long to say anything, I may just not say anything as it is easier. I sometimes miss the punchlines and people haven't got a clue what I'm talking about. You try to explain yourself when you can't talk or move. It is normally easier just to leave people clueless.

Over time I've learnt all the tricks which people use not to communicate with me. Some people avoid looking at my eyes. That way they can just say, "Oh, I didn't notice".

Also there are the people who ask other people to talk to me. There are the people who ask me questions and they don't even look at me when I answer. I don't answer people anymore if they can't be bothered to look at me. There are people who are impatient: they only let me say a word or half a sentence, then they simply presume that they know what I'm talking about. I now think very carefully about what I am going to say. "Can I paint my nails tomorrow?" becomes "Tomorrow can I paint my nails?" People don't always wait for the "tomorrow" and may start painting my nails that instant. There are the people who take one look at the letter board and run off saying that they can't do it - I think, "You haven't even tried". There are people who try to guess a word. As I spell out every letter this is OK, but some people guess repeatedly and accompany it with ums and ahs. I don't mind people guessing but when someone guesses loads of times on one letter, saying one sentence can take forever. It is much quicker to just let me spell what I want to say.

Chapter 6

My father

My father borrowed a wheelchair from the hospital with lots of pillows for support. I was able to go out. There was a lake outside my window which my father pushed me around. I remember the warm mornings in the spring and summertime and I could hear the quacking of the little ducklings. Also, during those hot mornings I would get the smell of freshly cut grass.

If it wasn't for my father taking me out, I would probably have been stuck inside that hospital for five and a half months. At the centre of the lake was a small island with trees, bushes and grass. During the warmer months the birds would go there to nest and for their safety. My father and I would look for the heron that would visit the lake. The heron would always stand on one leg like a flamingo. I spent many hours watching the life on the lake thinking about how lucky I was to witness such natural beauty. My father and I went out no matter what the weather was like. Of course, if it was really windy or raining outside, then we would simply go under the shelter to get some fresh air.

It was on one of our walks around the lake and with the communication board that I was able to have a chat about how I felt before my accident, that I felt that I was a disappointment to my family. How I felt like the black sheep. How I felt unloved by my family. I was always independent and was left to do my own thing. I felt so lonely. It was a long chat and one that we should have had long before we did. I didn't know how long I had left to live and I had to say how I felt. My father told me how proud of me my parents really were. I realised that I had wasted all those years being angry and all that I had to do was talk to my parents.

Being outside was refreshing. I could feel the breeze on my face. Being outside meant I could still hear the machines in the hospital beeping but not as loud. I could go outside with oxygen. I had an oxygen canister connected to my tracheostomy via a tube.

When I was alone in my room I remember most of the stupid activities the staff gave me to keep me occupied. My father brought in a TV to watch so I wouldn't be bored. Some of the staff would turn the television on but not tune it in so all I could see was four little pictures dancing around the screen. Another thing people did was turn the television on but leave me facing in a different direction so I couldn't see it. No-one read to me so I didn't have a clue what was going on in the world.

I remember sleeping a lot. I had nothing better to do and I guess it was my body's way of repairing itself. My inner thermostat was not working properly due to my fit. I remember waking up in a pool of sweat. I had never suffered from excessive sweating before and I had two fans on me.

I don't remember most of the time I was ill but I remember having a painful thrush in my throat and being given orange-flavoured medicine. When I was admitted to hospital, I was given a catheter. Most people with Locked-in Syndrome have no bladder control. I never imagined I'd ever have a catheter, especially at such a young age. My body didn't like it and I kept getting urine infections. The pain was excruciating; every wave of pain was like a contraction. I pushed and after a while my catheter would pop out. The pain would go instantly and the catheter had to be changed.

My father told hospital staff to check for a urine infection. The staff wanted me to wait for the doctor who was doing his rounds in the morning but reluctantly they did a urine test. The nurse removed my catheter and replaced it with a fresh one. The pain went almost instantly.

I don't remember all of my ailments from hospital but I remember that my jaw would sometimes lock and my top teeth would bite into my chin. My chin would bleed and it would really hurt. There was nothing I could do to stop myself.

I remember near the end of my stay that whenever I laid on my back, I got a pain in my ankle. The nurse told me I had developed foot drop. This is when a person spends too long in bed and their foot goes down like a ballerina's.

Chapter 7

Out of my control

One day my father came into my room with tears rolling down his face. I don't think I had ever seen my father cry before. I looked at him curiously. "It's your daughter", he began. Horror struck through me as I began to imagine all the scenarios that could involve my daughter. My father explained that she had been taken into care because she had become violent towards my nephew. My sister had not been able to cope so she had simply refused to collect her from school. My daughter was taken into foster care. I knew that she would be safe but I was annoyed that no-one had spoken to me before making such a drastic decision. I didn't have a child so that she would be taken into care but I knew that I was unable to take care of her myself and was glad that someone else was looking after her. I missed her so much. I was frustrated to not be able to make a decision about my own child. I couldn't even scream in frustration. I just had to accept other people's decisions.

I was given a psychology test. I was very depressed and was prescribed anti-depressants. Before my accident I had sworn that I would never take them and that I was strong enough to get through anything. I felt so sad and kept crying and I found it so difficult to crack a smile. Normally I would be smiling most of the time and I didn't think it was possible to feel so low. I felt guilty for not being with my child. I hated that my parents had to see me in such a state. I had always been very independent, active and confident. In an instant it was as though my feelings had been taken from me.

My worst nightmare came true whilst I was still in hospital. I got a visit from a person from social services who said, "Your daughter wants to see her father and he wants to see her." The social worker asked me how I felt about that. I was initially upset and very angry. I thought "Trust him to wait until I couldn't talk or move until he rears his ugly little head". We lived with my daughter's father until she was fifteen months old, then, for reasons I'm not allowed to discuss, I moved into a flat with my daughter. I was told by social services not to let my daughter see him or I would risk losing her. I did as social services wanted and never heard from him again. I did walk past him once. He had his arm around his pregnant girlfriend and he looked straight at me but he did not act as though he recognised me. My daughter ran straight past him. As I looked at him I had no feelings for him, I simply felt sorry for his girlfriend. She reminded me of me a few years before. But my daughter wanted to meet her father and, no matter what my feelings were towards him, I didn't want to stand in the way of her seeing him. I had once watched a talk show and the host was talking about fathers meeting their offspring. The host said that the fathers should be given enough rope to run with or to hang themselves with. This is what I had to do. I had to stand back and let my daughter meet him and let him make up for all the years he had missed.

Being in hospital was not all doom and gloom. At the beginning I didn't like men. I had a male speech therapist - whenever he spoke to me I would stare up at the ceiling and he presumed that I didn't understand and couldn't communicate. He had been very patronising to me prior to me ignoring him. All the female staff that worked with me argued with him saying that I could communicate so he looked stupid and as though he couldn't do his job properly.

On the positive side I became closer to my parents and I realised where I get my clumsiness from. My father was always tripping over things. Also, I caught up on Hollyoaks and Eastenders and I had a male nurse who regularly told me the time and the date and spoke to me properly, not in a tone which most people adopted when speaking to a child.

I am not a religious person. Some people would call me an atheist, but others may call me a non-believer. I don't mind what people call me, I just don't believe in any god. This does not mean that I am against anyone who does believe in religion, in fact I am a bit jealous that others have the faith to keep them strong if times get hard. Two nurses asked if they could pray for me. I kept thinking, "Do I look that bad?" but I looked up and thought, "Well, I'll try anything once". The two nurses placed their hands on my head and together quietly began to recite a prayer. I could not tell you what they were saying.

After five and a half months in the hospital I received confirmation that I would be moving. A night nurse explained to me that the hospital could not make me any better. I had improved from when I had first gone into hospital so I was ready for my next journey.

Chapter 8

Moving to my first care home

The day finally came. I was given an injection to stop me from being travel sick on my over four-hour ambulance trip. My body shook uncontrollably whilst the liquid went into my system. This is a normal response, said a nurse. My whole family, including my daughter, had turned up to wish me good luck. I smiled goodbye to the staff as I was wheeled past them on a stretcher. I remember my daughter shouting "Goodbye Mummy" as I went into the ambulance. How I wanted to say goodbye back. As I travelled, I could only see the rooftops and the trees. I remember an ambulance man put on one of my CDs to prevent me from being so bored on the journey. I soon arrived and the place was nothing like I expected. I had never been inside a residential care home before so I only had my imagination to go by. I expected all the patients to be in one room lined up like in a ward. Instead, all the patients had their own rooms and only met together in the communal area.

I presumed that there would be a lot of people with my condition so that I would have someone to relate to but the only person that had Locked-in Syndrome was an eighty-year-old man and I couldn't relate to him because he had different life experiences.

As I cannot walk, I am transferred using a sling and hoist. The sling is a piece of material which has some tags coming off from it. The sling attaches to the hoist. The hoist is a strong piece of metal machinery used by carers to get me from one place to another. On the day that I moved I had a bath. I was hoisted in my chair naked using a mesh sling that is designed for the bath. I was covered with old towels and wheeled into the bathroom where the towels were removed. There was a hoist in the bathroom and I was lifted into the bath. I could hear the bubbles as they popped against my skin. The bubbles popping sounded like footsteps on a pile of autumn leaves. As the warm water enveloped my body a smile grew across my face. It was not like having a normal bath but, as I had not been in the bath for five and a half months, to me it was like heaven. While I was in the bath I had my hair washed and my legs shaved. For a while it felt like me again.

Before I had gone to the bathroom I was put on my bed. There were two full-length mirrors on the wall at the foot of the bed. I had not seen my reflection since before my accident. Before, I was vain and was happy to see my reflection. My parents were with me the first time I saw myself. I was shocked. I was a model before my accident but I couldn't do modelling now. What was once a shapely face was now a shapeless, round face with a double chin. My abs were gone and I was left with a stomach with no muscle. I had worked so hard to make my muscles defined but now it was just a waste of my time. I once had muscly, shapely legs and I now had pasty, white, shapeless legs which did not do as I wanted. I cried seeing myself. Now I had to get used to a whole new body which I had not opted to have.

I know I should just be grateful to be alive and I am, but I can't help mourning for the girl I once was. I spoke to my father about my appearance. I felt so unattractive, looking at my reflection wasn't a good idea. "I am a minger", I said, "I will never get married." I had never dreamt of a big marriage and a big white dress but marriage would be nice one day. I did think I would live in a big house with a nice car and a good job. I never imagined I would be in a wheelchair.

Out in the fresh air

Chapter 9

Fighting pneumonia

That evening I couldn't breathe properly. I found it hard to take a breath and my chest was so painful. Every time I tried to breathe in, I coughed. Phlegm would come up with every cough and I was very hot. A doctor examined me and I was rushed into hospital with pneumonia. I didn't know much about pneumonia, I just knew someone who had died from it so I was petrified. Apparently pneumonia is common with people who have Locked-in Syndrome. I had fluid in my lungs. It probably got into my lungs when I had the bath.

I was given antibiotics which cleared up my lungs but they were a bit too strong for my stomach and I kept getting diarrhoea. Lovely. I wasn't even given an incontinence pad to wear. I think the theory was that every time I was changed, the bed was so soiled that to save materials they just left me without. I had a sheet covering me so at least people could not see what was going on beneath my sheet. My father moaned at some of the staff. I don't know how long I was supposed to sit in my own faeces but I got very sore. I thought that having a baby was undignified but this was worse. My daughter came to see me at the end of my stay in hospital. As usual she bounced up to my bed and seeing her filled me with joy. I was glad she couldn't see under my sheet. She hugged me and said, "I'm glad you didn't die Mummy". They were the most moving six words to me.

I hated being in hospital. It was here that I realised how important it was to have someone around me that knew me. Some of the staff did try but they had never used a communication board. Most people just presumed that because I couldn't speak I couldn't think.

I was so glad to see my parents; they could communicate and understand my needs. My father visited me every day whilst I was in hospital. The six-hour round trip was too much for my mother to make every day so she visited a few times a week.

On my first day my father came to visit me and I was in a right state. I had been given an incontinence pad which is like a giant nappy. My pad had not been changed so it was full of urine. I wondered if it exploded would it be filled with lots of tiny crystals like baby's nappies. My father found me hanging through the bed railing where I had coughed and unintentionally gone right through and no-one bothered to move me back. I was shaking with fear. My father informed someone that I was ready for my morning care. Over two hours later I was still waiting to be washed and changed.

I had a huge cocktail of drugs; I think if I could walk I would have rattled. A doctor came to see me to assess me, "Does it communicate?" he asked my father. "It does communicate with its eyes and it is a she and she is called Tracey", my father replied. He was so calm; I would have lost my temper.

My poor father. First, he had driven over three hours, then he had found me in a right state and now his youngest daughter was being referred to as an 'it'. Normally this kind of comment would have really hurt me but I think the anti-depressants were working. As these words spilled out of his mouth they didn't bother me. I just think people are naïve. Most people, even those in the medical profession, have not heard of Locked-in Syndrome, let alone met someone like me. So I understand people not knowing how to handle me, but I do ask that people read my file so that they know why I am the way I am.

I spent just over a week in hospital and I was given antibiotics through an intravenous drip so I had a needle in my hand. I had got used to having needles in me since being ill and called myself the human pin cushion. I don't remember all of how I felt while I had pneumonia but I slept a lot. I remember being suctioned and having chest physio at least twice a day. One day my father and one of my friends came to visit me. I went over some memories with them, some funny, some not so funny. I had to tell them that I didn't want to take those memories to the grave with me.

I got on well with one of my male nurses. He was good-looking but he was too much on the young side for me. Besides, I could look at a good-looking guy and just be friends with him. It was nice to have someone to look at even if I did scare him. I don't think he knew what to do. Before my accident I probably would have chewed him up and spat him out. He said he could come to work with his friend naked to raise money. I told him he should come to work naked anyway. I had not met a guy who was remotely good-looking or that was near to my age since I had had the accident. Before the accident I would have just said what I liked without thinking. My frankness was often misunderstood and it did get me into quite a lot of trouble. After my accident it was nice to feel that some of my old personality was still apparent. I just have to think a lot before I decide what to say.

Before my daughter had said "I'm glad you didn't die Mummy", I did think it would be better for everyone if I was not here anymore. I thought if everyone just mourned once for me instead of keep seeing me in hospital, it would be better. But I realised that my loved ones didn't mind what I looked like, they were just pleased to see me. My daughter showed me what was in her bag. She had come with her foster mother. I was grateful to her for looking after my daughter, but I was also very jealous. I knew I was in no fit state to look after a child, but I still wanted to be the one she kissed goodnight and the one to make her feel better when she hurt herself. I smiled as they left. I wanted to cry as I watched my daughter leave with another woman, but I did not show my true emotions as I did not want to upset her.

As the days went on I realised how much I normally use my arms. Little things like pushing the hair out of my eyes or scratching, to holding a book were just some of the actions I was unable to do anymore. I suddenly realised that there was not much which I could do. I had loads of time on my hands and nothing to do. I realised that this was about to be a very boring time.

Chapter 10

Living with Locked-in Syndrome

The hospital was so boring. There was nothing to do except watch the television. When I was admitted I had some swab tests taken which showed that I had MRSA in my system. The staff did not want the other patients to get it, understandably, so I was put in a room by myself. I couldn't even people watch!

Due to the Locked-in Syndrome I get a lot of eye infections. They are like having grit in your eye and they are horrible. I can't even rub my eyes or look at them in the mirror. I was prescribed some eye-drops in the hospital. They were put on the bin lid. Someone opened the bin using the foot pedal and as the lid opened the drops fell down the back of the bin next to the wall. For the next few days I watched some staff members scurry around looking for them but not once did someone ask me if I had seen them. In the end my father asked me if I knew where they were. If he had never asked me, I wonder if they would ever have found them.

Soon I was well enough to leave the hospital so I went back to the care home in an ambulance. I was greeted by the happy faces of the staff although I did not know them well. It was nice to see familiar faces. I was given a few days to settle back into my room. I had sores on my bum and on my left ear I had some bruises from the hospital. The staff at the home were surprised by the state of my skin. I was given a cream which healed my sores and my bruises went away on their own so in a few weeks my skin was back to its normal self.

I didn't sit in the lounge and watch television with the other residents because I was not interested in what was on television. Although I had a brain injury I still knew what I liked and disliked. Everyone told me I should socialise more. Not being able to talk or move meant that I found socialising difficult.

My daughter was not brought to see me for twelve weeks. I was fuming and I never did get an apology or an explanation as to why she wasn't coming. I just remember my disappointment as I waited for her and she never showed up. As the weeks went by I cried more and more. I missed her so much I was worried that she might forget me. I felt that I was being punished for being ill.

It was my father who informed social services about my lack of visits and they eventually sorted it out and that's when I finally saw my daughter again. She bounced in like normal. She had not forgotten me at all. She was aware that she hadn't seen me for twelve weeks and she was as angry as I was about it.

Before my accident I would drop my daughter off at school and I would go for a jog with my puppy. Then I would do my housework. This was all before midday. At the care home I got out of bed at about eleven o'clock in the morning when the staff were ready to get me up. That was one thing I missed, just waking up and jumping out of bed when I wanted to. Instead I would be woken up at about 5 o'clock in the morning for my medication, then I would just lie staring at the ceiling. I would normally go to bed for an afternoon nap as well. It was as if as soon as I got out of bed someone would ask me if I wanted to get back into bed. I would think I have just got up. I only slept for a few hours; I was wasting time really.

My television was switched on at about eleven in the morning and switched off about midnight. I even knew the order of the adverts in between programmes. I don't even like watching television and not once did I get asked if I actually enjoyed watching it.

I had physiotherapy for just twenty minutes, about once a week. This consisted of me pedalling and it was so boring. My feet were strapped to the pedals of the electric bike and the pedals went round as though I was controlling the bike. I'm surprised that my muscles stayed supple at all.

I did cookery because it was something to do even though it was so boring as all I could do was watch. My father was a trained chef so I knew how to cook well but the carer who did cookery with me did not have a clue what she was doing. Luckily, like me, my father found the funny side of it and did not show his anger or frustration.

When the weather was OK my parents would take me out around the grounds. I loved being outside and the grounds were very nice but they were built on a hill so wherever my parents went they had to push me and my wheelchair up a hill.

I love the beach - it is my thinking spot. I find the sound of the crashing waves soothing and I love the crunch of stones beneath people's feet. I even like the squawk from seagulls.

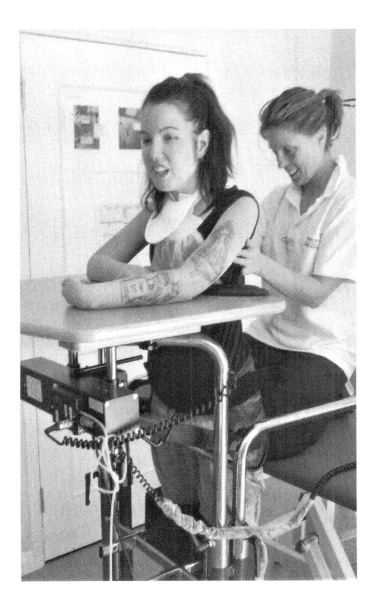

Me with the physiotherapist

Chapter 11

A different area

I had gone back to the care home in Wiltshire. I could hear all the birds and they were very different to what I was used to. I could tell I was inland and in a different part of the country because there were just fields as far as the eye could see. I was used to the squawking of seagulls and the cooing of pigeons but instead I could hear knocking from woodpeckers. They sound a bit like someone hammering. I could also hear the sound of a cockerel in the neighbouring farm. It sounded as though it was being strangled. Instead of going cock-a-doodle-do it went cock-a-doodle arghhhh! It did make me laugh.

As the weather improved so did my health. I was able to stay awake for a bit longer. I felt a little stronger. My daughter came to visit me. I was doing my physio at the time. She loved helping me and seeing me get better and she was asked to tell me to move my head. I did what I was instructed. I still wanted to be indestructible mummy who could do anything.

She then asked my physiotherapist the one question a child should never have to ask: what happened to my Mummy? How is that explained to a six-year old? "Your Mummy has a brain injury", said the physiotherapist. I guess that is the best way to explain it to a young child. It was the simplest way to tell a child. How I wanted to sit her down and explain to her what had happened myself.

I soon finished the physio session. My daughter wheeled me back to my room. She loved pushing my wheelchair. I think that pushing me made her feel important, like she was doing something to help. I only let her push as she was tall for her age. Her father is six foot two inches and I am nearly five foot eight so she was bound to end up tall. I would not have let her push me if I did not think she could manage.

My daughter sat in my room for a bit talking. She was only six years old. Then she just left the room and I could hear her sobbing in the hallway. One of her carers was trying to calm her. I wanted to hug her and tell her that everything would be OK. Instead I had to sit in my wheelchair and listen to her cry. She was taken home and no-one even told me that she had gone home or mentioned that she had been crying. She was brought to see me a fortnight later and no-one mentioned what happened the fortnight before.

I felt very lonely. I was miles from everyone and everything I knew. My work mates came to see me at the care home. They treated me like they always had. They realised that I still had my sense of humour and they told me what was happening in my home town. One of my friends got married but I couldn't go as I was too ill. All of my friends turned up in their bridesmaids dresses and my friend who got married turned up in her wedding dress. They didn't want me to feel left out so they brought the wedding to me.

My friend who got married also had a hen do. Everyone dressed up as gangsters and they all wore white trilby hats. I loved hats and I loved wearing trilby hats.

I expected to see the same people who I had seen before my accident. They were the ones who said that they would stick around if something happened to me, but I never saw some of them again. I guess it's true what they say, that you don't know who your friends are until something major happens. No-one prepares you for this. I just expected my friends to support me.

There are people who don't realise I have changed. Some people say I bet you miss nicotine and say they will blow smoke in my face. I don't miss smoking, in fact I find the smell vile. If someone blows smoke in my face I will probably choke and die. My lungs are not as strong as they used to be.

I can't wear short skirts or dresses because I will probably accidentally end up flashing my knickers. I can't wear heels, not that I used to wear them much anyway, but it is nice to have the option. I have foot drop. If I wear heels my foot gets held up in a position where my toes go down and my heel goes up, so my foot drop gets worse.

My neck muscles are not very strong so I have a headrest on my wheelchair. This means that I have to be careful which style I have my hair. It is very uncomfortable leaning on a ponytail. I also have to be careful what hats I wear. I wear hats to keep the sun off my eyes but, because of where my headrest sits, a lot of hats can't be worn.

Every time I go over a bump, my hat and glasses need readjusting. My hat tends to fall down over my eyes or it goes backwards. When the sun is shining in my eyes a nice stroll becomes a frustrating, time-consuming venture out. I can't just pop out; I have to plan everything. I have to ensure that there are enough trained staff to go with me and, most important of all, I have to ensure that the venue I am going to is wheelchair accessible. Wheelchairs and stairs don't go together very well. These are just little things I never imagined I would have to think about.

My first trip out was to Stonehenge. I didn't know how ignorant people could be. Some people walked right in front of my chair and some people bashed right into me. It was as though I was invisible. My parents, main carer, another carer and my OT came with me. I was glad that they had all come with me as I needed their emotional support. I was OK with my condition but I was not ready for the public's reaction to a disabled person. I learnt to look down and avoid everyone else's looks. Some people stare, some people point and some don't look at me at all. I would much rather people came up to me and asked, "Why are you in that wheelchair?", but I understand people not asking me as they may be embarrassed. I remember being that person who wouldn't look at disabled people so I didn't appear rude, now I know that what I was doing was very rude.

I went round Stonehenge. It was nice, just not as exciting as I thought it would be. I don't know what I was expecting, maybe dancing monkeys. I realise that it wasn't the attraction that was boring, it was me. I couldn't prance around. I couldn't point at something and say "Oh, look, that's nice". Instead I just sat in my wheelchair and looked at the attraction. I went to the gift shop, of course everything had Stonehenge written on it so when I was asked what I wanted I said a stone! They spent ages looking for a stone before they realised I was joking. We got back to the minibus and it poured down with rain, we had just missed getting wet.

Chapter 12

The move to improve

My first venture out since my accident had gone OK. When I first became ill, I didn't want to live as a disabled person. At first I got very upset and I didn't want to go any further. I was so busy focussing on what I couldn't do instead of focussing on what I could. I was crying one day when my keyworker said, "Your life isn't over, it's just different". She was right and from that moment I saw my life through different eyes. I realised that with the right care and understanding life is not so bad. There is a note in my care plan saying that if anything happens to me then not to revive me. It is

OK being like this but I don't want to be any worse and I don't want to go through this all over again.

I was embarrassed that I now had to do my business in an incontinence pad. I felt like a small child weeing in a nappy. I was embarrassed by the smell and was quite relieved that my main carer had something wrong with her sinuses so she had no sense of smell. It was just one less thing for me to worry about.

My carer finally asked me the one question I had been waiting for someone to ask me for months. "Do you know when you need to go the toilet?", she asked. "Yes", I answered. Again, "Can you stop yourself from going?" and I answered "Yes". I didn't know how I did it as my pelvic floor muscles didn't seem to work. From then on I didn't have to wear a pad during the day, I used a bedpan instead. It was presumed that because I had Locked-in Syndrome I couldn't control my bladder. No-one had bothered to ask me. Never just presume anything.

Along came summer and with it came flying insects. I hadn't thought that because I was paralysed I couldn't get them off. So they crawled on my skin and there was nothing I could do to make them fly away. I remember one crawled on my face for ages. I closed my eyes and mouth and hoped that the insect would not crawl up my nose. It didn't, it flew away instead. Relief came over me.

That year my friends came to see me and they were getting browner and browner. I normally tan well but for the first time ever I was too ill to stay outside. Summer came and I stayed white. I did get to sit outside in my wheelchair occasionally. On one of these occasions a family in the same area as me were visiting one of the other residents. There was a little girl who was only about two years old. She tugged at her Mum's sleeve pointing at me and said, "Look,

Mummy, she is dead". I suppose to everyone else I did look dead. I was white and not moving so it was easy to come to that conclusion. I looked dead.

As the summer deteriorated, so did my health. I ended up in hospital again because I had difficulty breathing. I had a chest infection so I was put on antibiotics and given oxygen. I remember I had a lot of medication. I had never seen so much except in a chemist's. As I watched out of my window I could see some army men practising combat in a nearby field. I remember sleeping a lot. I was so bored that my parents read me stories from a magazine and I looked forward to when my parents or friends visited. It was the time I got on well with two physiotherapists. They saw me about twice a day. They talked to me as though I was normal.

I remember my father came in once and he went to take a paper towel from a pile on the side. Unbeknown to my father most of the towels were stuck together so as he took one they all came with him like a paper chain. I burst out laughing and my father's face was a picture. I had not lost my sense of humour, I could still laugh and smile, it was just more difficult now. I was a little less serious and I found things funny which I had never found funny before. I used to be able to control my laughing but now if I find something funny I can't help but to laugh.

By this point I had been in hospital for about four weeks. Every night I was meant to wear splints on my legs to prevent me from getting foot drop but, while I was in the hospital, I didn't have my splints so my foot drop got worse. I'd not had a toileting accident since I'd become ill but, in the hospital, I said that I needed a bedpan and I was kept waiting for ages. By the time the bedpan came it was too late and I had wet myself. The staff got me changed but didn't pull my trousers up properly so as I was hoisted the staff got a view of my behind.

Luckily I do not embarrass easily. I had physio afterwards so I was hoisted onto my bed. The care staff left and some overwhelming emotions washed over me. I burst out crying. I was comforted by my physiotherapist. She said it was the straw that broke the camel's back and I think she was right. I had always been like that. I'm a bit like a rubber band; I can be stretched and stretched and then I just snap. Then I calm down as quickly as I flare up.

A doctor said that I was well enough to go back to the care home as long as my oxygen stayed up at a certain level. Every time I got wheezy my oxygen machine got turned up. I was supposed to get chest physio or suction if I got wheezy but this never happened so my oxygen got higher and higher and because of this I was not allowed to leave the hospital even though I was feeling better. This happened over and over again. My father complained to the staff but it made no difference so he went higher and wrote a letter to someone in the management. He said that if I was not discharged soon then he would discharge me himself and arrange transport. Finally, my father was listened to and my oxygen got lower and lower. I was discharged and allowed to leave the hospital.

My new home was a neurological rehabilitation unit which means that all the residents have a brain injury. Everyone has their own problems. Most people had trouble communicating so no-one could communicate with me and this meant that it was difficult to make friends. I was lonely and bored. I was far away from anyone and everyone that I knew. Some of my friends came to see me, which was nice, but it was a long way for people to travel.

My parents visited me every week, which kept me sane. It was quite nice not knowing anyone. I wasn't sure how people would react to my appearance so I was glad that I could recuperate without bumping into anyone I knew. I had a day out shopping, which I loved. It felt nice to do something I enjoyed doing. I have always loved clothes and just because I'm disabled this hasn't changed. I have lots of clothes. I love the satisfaction of buying clothes and knowing that they are mine. Using the letter board I was able to choose what I wanted. My father was with me and I was quite lucky because he knows what I like so he can show me something in a shop which I might want to buy. He won't show me some garments I will never wear so it saves a lot of time.

Along came November and along came my birthday. Summer had gone away and what a boring summer it had been. I had spent most of my time asleep or in front of the television. The illness and medication had made me very tired and I don't think I have slept so much in my life. On my birthday my friends visited me bearing gifts, which was nice, but I found my birthday a miserable day. It was my first year of being ill and so it was my first year away from my home town and from my daughter. I missed her so much.

In December 2008 I moved to a place in Tonbridge. I was closer to my home in Hastings and there was more for me to do there. I really thought my life would improve. I thought that by some miracle I would get better as quickly as I had become ill. I didn't know what to expect.

Chapter 13

Relationships

When I got the news about my up-and-coming move, I was so happy. I was told that I would get better and be able to walk out of there after six months. I was genuinely excited, thinking that I could have part of my old life back again. I was moving to another brain injury unit in Tonbridge. I would be staying in a building in the grounds for six weeks so that I could be assessed. I hadn't seen the place but it was closer to my daughter. I had been told on good authority that it was a nice place to live. There were people who had the type of brain injuries which affect their thoughts.

When I lived at the care home in Tonbridge, I definitely had lots of eye-openers. First, my key worker put an opened bottle of my liquid feed on the wooden footrest at the end of my bed. She quickly turned round whilst talking. She flung her arms out expressing herself as she spoke. She knocked over the bottle and sticky liquid got spilt everywhere. The feed covered everything. My carer and I just laughed.

I moved to this new care home a year after my accident and spent 21 months there. Some people would like it but I hated being there. The man who owned the home when I lived there didn't like any electrical items. I had no television. The man who made the stupid rule would then tell me about programmes he was watching. Maybe he thought he was being nice but it was just cruel. A friend who was in his late 20s had his mobile phone confiscated. I only knew people of school age who had belongings taken away. When you are paralysed you can't do anything alone so unless you get one-to-one care you need to rely on electrical goods for entertainment. Also, there is a lot of technology that helps with my disabilities.

I was not allowed any electrical equipment so I was very bored. I just presumed that being disabled was really boring. I didn't think that I would ever be happy living as a disabled person but I was wrong. Yes, I get frustrated and would prefer not to be disabled, but it is amazing how the body adapts to change. It is non-disabled people who believe that being disabled is awful. Years ago there would not have been the medical knowledge that exists today, so most people wouldn't survive the initial trauma.

All relationships are very different since I became disabled. I haven't seen my so-called best friend for over two years. I used to go to her house nearly every day for more than six years. We even agreed that if one of us was in a coma the other person would shave the legs of the person in the coma so that they wouldn't wake up with gorilla legs. I never thought of a future where she was not in it. I woke up with hairy legs and didn't care. I felt very different to how I thought I would feel. I bet you are reading this and saying to yourself that your best friend will never leave you. Ten years ago I would have said exactly the same. I'm still friends with some of my friends that I used to know and I treasure the people who stuck around. They are now my closest friends.

My relationships with my parents changed. My father was with me nearly every day. He stayed with me every time I had a medical treatment. My father was my voice and my arms. My parents broke up when I had been ill for about five years. They had been a couple for thirty-five years. I don't believe they broke up because of me but having a disabled person in the family would put a strain on any family.

Chapter 14

My world

This care home was the first place where I had encountered people who spoke in a different language to me. I was lying in my bed and a male nurse came in to give me an injection. He said, "Here comes a little prick". I started laughing and spelt out to my father, "I've had a few of them." We started laughing but the nurse stayed straight-faced. I don't think he knew what I was laughing at.

I was so bored at this care home. I could feel my confidence slipping away so I asked to move. I wanted to be around people who spoke English and I wanted to be closer to my friends and family.

After a year of lying in my bed every evening, staring up at a plain ceiling, I was bored stiff. I had quite a few audio books which I listened to, to keep my mind occupied, but I had no way of contacting anybody and after a while I found the audio books boring.

Having no television made things seem worse. I have never been a big television watcher but when I became paralysed I worked out that I had to keep myself occupied with hobbies led by sight or sound.

I'd had enough. I made an appointment to meet with the owner. It was time for me to give him an ultimatum. Either give me a television or I will leave. A care home is just a business. They get over a grand a week for every patient. Within just a few days I was moved to a room in the main house. Here I was allowed a television and I was told that I would never get bored. I was so excited and I get itchy feet so I've never stayed long in a job or a home.

I happily moved to the main house. I had a shower not a bath and there were free-standing hoists and not ceiling hoists. These are just two compromises I had to make in order to move.

My parents viewed the care home before I went there to ensure that it was a suitable place for me. They were informed that it was not a religious place. What a load of rubbish! I actually got told that I fell ill because I don't believe in God! I am an atheist. On all the walls were pictures showing scenes and characters from the Bible.

Once a week a priest would come and perform a communion with the residents. One day I went along just for something to do and to see what it was like. There was a talk about God and then the priest tried to put some bread and wine in my mouth. I kept my mouth closed and turned my head away. I was 'nil by mouth'. If I had anything orally I could have choked and died!

I wasn't allowed to hang any of my personal pictures in my room in case I ruined any of the special and expensive paint. My father used to own his own painting and decorating business. He checked out the paint for me and it was normal, standard paint.

Once, my parents and I got told that we had to attend an extremely important meeting. Everyone was squeezed like sardines into a room that was too small, ready for the meeting. The big boss man turned on the projector. Then he began his speech. For about five minutes he waffled on about a story that is in the Bible. I exchanged a look of help with my father. He knowingly asked, "Do you want to leave?" I smiled and looked up to say "Yes". My parents stood up ready to leave. "Sit down and shut up", barked the big boss man to my father. "Big mistake", I thought. I had never heard anybody speak to my father like that. "Do you still want to leave?", my father asked me. I said yes. "Sorry but she wants to leave", my father announced. There were loads of chairs in front of us so we left backwards, out of the patio doors and into the garden. A few people left after me.

I made some gingerbread men when I lived at the care home but I misread the recipe. I put a tablespoonful of ginger in the biscuits but I was supposed to put a teaspoonful in. A tablespoon is equal to four teaspoons. I gave a biscuit to my father and just looked on and tried to stay poker-faced and not laugh. At first everything was fine. He chewed it. Fine. He swallowed. At first he was fine, then his throat got hotter and hotter and he needed a drink. I burst out laughing.

Chapter 15

Struggling with foot drop

I suffered from foot drop, which basically means that my ankle muscles weren't working properly so my feet faced downwards. The staff were determined to get the feet facing the right way. I was told that my ankles were more pliable when they were hot so I was given a hot sulphur footbath about five times a week. I dreaded these because they stank out my room, me and the corridor! Sulphur smells like rotten eggs so I regularly put my feet into a bucket of hot water that stank of bad eggs. Mmm, very relaxing, not.

The staff then pushed on the soles of my feet trying to get them to point the correct way. After this the physio would put me on the tilt table and I would be standing up for about half an hour. My body weight would add pressure to my ankles, forcing my feet to point the correct way. It hurt. If I complained I would be quoted, "No pain, no gain". Luckily I don't weigh a huge amount.

I was also made to wear some foot splints to encourage my feet to point the correct way. The splints were made from the same material that a cast is made from. They were moulded and made whilst on my feet. When the splints were dry the physio used special scissors to cut them off my feet. All was fine until he got to the angle where my ankle goes into my foot. Then with every movement of the scissors he would unknowingly stab my foot and I wanted to punch him. I remember I kept pulling my foot away in pain. He angrily told me to keep still and I remember thinking to myself,

"I would keep still if you didn't keep hurting me." He must have noticed by my facial expression that I was being serious and that I was actually in pain. After about a year of putting up with that pain, the heat and the bad smell, my feet lifted by about a centimetre or two. Was it worth it? No.

The surgeon later suggested that I had a tendon release operation to fix my foot drop. Locked-in Syndrome is rare and the anaesthetists always worried about me having a general anaesthetic. I don't know why they worry. Nothing bad has ever happened to me when I have had an anaesthetic.

I was under general anaesthetic for the operation and when I awoke I had hard casts on both my feet. I only stayed in hospital for a night. Back at the care home I slept for a day and then had to sit outside with my parents just to get some fresh air. My legs were both jerking in and I was in so much pain and I was sweating. My parents spoke to my nurse about getting some stronger painkillers. I took the pills and felt better. But after a day my feet had swollen up and I was in agony so I was taken back to hospital. They split open my casts at the front and the pain went immediately. A few weeks went past and I had to go back to hospital just to have my casts renewed. We found that due to my feet moving because of the pain I had rubbed my heels down to the bone. It took a whole year for my heels to get better. Within that year I was seen by a local tissue viability nurse. I tried lots of different dressings and I even had vacuum packs on each heel. For that year I could not wear shoes. I just told myself that a day or a month or a year are all just short periods in the length of my life.

One year I had an ingrowing hair which was on my lower back, which needed to be cut out. This time the surgeon worried about how I would react to anaesthetic so I had to have a local anaesthetic. I was numbed from the waist down. I remember I was worried that I might wet myself and there was nothing that I could do to stop myself. I was awake for the operation and it was being shown on a screen so I could watch if I wanted. I didn't watch. I don't like gory things so I stared at one spot on the wall but soon the operation was over and the wound was treated with manuka honey.

My birthday party in a balloon castle

Chapter 16

Being me

There were good points for being at the care home in Tonbridge. A few of the staff did understand what I was saying and so they were able to delve more into my personality and have a joke with me.

The grounds in the springtime were absolutely beautiful. In my room there were lots of windows and a set of double patio doors which led to the grounds outside. As the sunshine streamed in through my windows I could hear the birds singing in the trees. It was as though someone had painted the ground a purple-blue colour.

The ground was awash with bluebells. These were my grandad's favourite flower. So by looking out at them I felt as though I was close to my grandad.

The girls I used to work with would visit me quite regularly. They would drive all the way from Hastings to Tonbridge. They were always happy and never complained. They joked around and treated me like they always had. I have always been very grateful to them for supporting me and not disappearing out of my life like so many people had. They called themselves the crazy gang. They were funny and loud and I suppose compared to a lot of people they come across as a little bit crazy. They are the best people I have ever met.

I remember on my 28th birthday they all visited me bearing gifts. The biggest gift was a blow-up man. He had bright orange hair and instead of a hairy chest he had a hairy belly! I laughed when I opened the gift. My friends told me that he was to keep me company. I called him George and wherever I went that day George came with me. We went for a walk in the vast grounds. In the far corner was some woodland. I had never been in those particular woods so I was curious. My friends took me into the woods and down a very cracked and bumpy path. When we reached the bottom of the path all we could see was overgrown woodland. There was a pond to my right but I couldn't see the water through all of the yellow, fallen leaves that lay on the pond. Now we had to worry about getting back up the hill. The ground was cracked and bumpy and full of twigs. Luckily we all saw the funny side. We all laughed as my friends pushed and pulled my wheelchair back up the path.

One day my friends all visited me. One friend came out of my shared bathroom clutching an unusually shaped object. "I like this vase" she announced, whilst holding it up like a trophy. One of my other friends started laughing and said, "That's a man's pee bottle". "Ooh", announced my friend. She held the bottle away from her body and quickly put it back in the bathroom. They always made me laugh when they visited.

The move into the main house happened after just a couple of days. I still went to the small house for some of my therapies. I was told that chiropractice would be useful for me so it was put on my activities timetable. I don't know the effect of chiropractice on the body, I just did it. In chiropractice the bed is not very wide and I am only skinny so one day I was lying on the bed during my treatment when I gave an almighty cough and my body jerked and I moved. I fell off the bed and landed on my carer who had positioned herself between me and the floor. We all looked at each other and then we burst out laughing. We must have looked a right picture because my carer was about five foot whereas I am nearly five foot eight inches.

Chapter 17

Out and about

I had now been at the residential care home in Tonbridge for over a year and I had done their therapies repeatedly with no significant improvement. I didn't find a huge number of things to keep me occupied and the therapies didn't appear to be improving my health so I refused to continue them. I was told that if I did all my therapies for two weeks then I would get a special trip out. So I would get a special trip for doing what I had been doing for months anyway. I did all my therapies like a good girl! After just two weeks I excitedly awaited my special trip. A couple of carers came to take me on the trip. I had the peak of my cap covering my face. This was to keep the sunshine out of my eyes and also to hide my face from strangers. My confidence was really low and I still hadn't accepted that I was disabled. We went down a few paths and through a few alleyways. Soon we reached our destination. I peered out from underneath my cap. In front of me stood a vast, grey brick building. On closer inspection I could see that it was a library. Yep, I had an exciting trip to the local library! Since my accident I suffered from staggered vision. This meant that reading was very difficult for me so although it was just nice to be out of the unit, it wasn't exactly a fun day out.

The grounds of the care home were massive. Every Sunday my father used to take me outside. We were told that we should stay in the grounds but I would not be confined to one area, when the illness was confining enough. Especially during the summer months I used to go to the local newsagents. There I'd purchase a scratch card and a lollipop. We'd then sit under a tree and watch the children playing in a field. I dreamt I was watching my own child play and laugh. I would suck the flavour from the lollipop. I wasn't able to eat but I could still taste things. Eventually I headed back to the house. If the staff ever asked where I had been my father would say we were just walking within the grounds. The grounds were so large you could easily get lost in them.

On most days, however, I just sat in my bedroom with only a radio station to keep me company. I was ridiculously bored. One spring day there was an open day across the road from the care home. On the poster advertising the event it said that it was wheelchair friendly. And yes there were no steps but I wouldn't quite class it as wheelchair friendly! The ground was damp from the dewdrops in the morning and the grassland was uneven and up a hill. The pathways were gravel, which looks nice but if you have ever pushed a wheelchair on loose stones, you'd know that it is extremely difficult. At the open day there were no large animals like sheep or cows, just smaller animals like ferrets and piglets. On the back of every wheelchair there are two little wheels which are used to prevent the wheelchair from tipping over backwards. When I got back to the care home my wheels were covered in mud and my safety wheels had come off.

There weren't many trips out at this place but once I went to a zoo. The problem was it was a cold and grey day and as I moved around the zoo there were wide, wooden handrails around each enclosure. The railings were at my eye height so I couldn't see inside the enclosures! In most of them I could only see the middle bit of the animal and I couldn't move my head to see what the rest of the animal looked like. I didn't have any trouble seeing the larger animals like the giraffes or the elephants.

I became really miserable when I lived at the care home in Tonbridge. My confidence was lower than it had ever been. I was quite vain before my accident but now I couldn't even look at my reflection without crying. The girl looking at me was not the girl I was used to. I didn't see any improvement to my health. I hadn't accepted that I was disabled and I certainly hadn't accepted the way that people were treating me. A lot of people would talk to me very loudly and slowly as though I was a bit deaf or stupid. I am neither but I do find it rather offensive that someone would just presume that I was a bit deaf or stupid just because I am disabled.

Some people who I had known for years disappeared and never spoke to me again. I thought that I had done something wrong to them. I thought that maybe I looked so bad that people couldn't stand looking at me! Well, I didn't like looking at me so I thought why would anybody else?

I really missed my daughter. I cried every week because I wanted to be with my little girl. Instead I was stuck in a place that I hated.

I had put on some weight and this made me miserable. If anybody else had put on a lot of weight I would not have been disgusted by them yet why did I feel judged by others? I ballooned from a dress size 6 to 8 to a dress size 14 to 16. I knew that I needed to put on some weight but to jump up so many dress sizes was too much for me. I hated my situation.

I occasionally went and sat with the other residents in the dining room. Bear in mind that most other residents had frontal lobe damage so they couldn't control the things they did. There was a man. I think he was in his late forties. He would stand in the dining room and shout "I love you" repeatedly.

There was a woman. Again she seemed to be in her forties. From a distance you would not have guessed that she had brain damage. She would always sit in the same place at the same table. On this particular day she sat at that table. She drank her tea and ate her biscuits. Then she bent down, removed her knickers and put them on the table! But part of my condition is to laugh uncontrollably so I found the woman and her knickers hilarious. Sitting in a room with people who suffered from a form of brain damage and who can't control their actions looked amusing. Don't worry, I laughed at my own actions too.

Sara brought her wedding dress to show me

Chapter 18

Being locked in

Some people wanted proof in writing that I am mentally capable so I went to do a mental capacity test with a Professor Barbara Wilson. It took a few weeks to complete. I enjoyed doing the test. It was nice having something to do that stimulated the brain.

After a while I got my results and, as I had predicted, my brain was functioning normally. In fact my memory is better than most people's. I was given a list of sixteen items to remember. More than five years have passed and I can still remember at least ten items from the list!

The manager of the care home in Tonbridge had changed my diagnosis so it appeared that I had frontal lobe damage and was totally incapable of making a decision. Anyone that knew me could see that this was not true. Thankfully the test showed that the thinking part of my brain was functioning fine. My diagnosis was changed back to Locked-in Syndrome and my file said that I was totally capable of making a decision.

Whilst I was still living in Tonbridge, I was very surprised by what I saw. The man who owned the home mainly employed foreign workers and gave the staff a shared flat that went with the job, but it wasn't a great flat and the owner would sack people for no apparent reason. The staff were petrified about losing their jobs and ending up homeless. He doesn't own the care home anymore.

One day one resident was annoyed by another. The annoying resident lived in the room next to mine. I had just had a shower so I was lying on my bed and I was naked whilst two carers were drying me. The annoying resident was screaming. The other man was wielding a knife. My neighbour screamed which only annoyed the other resident even more. The man who had the knife flung open my door. He mumbled something about him getting the wrong room and then left whilst apologising profusely. One of my carers had run into my ensuite bathroom and my other carer had ducked down behind the bed. Imagine if he had gone for me! I was paralysed and unable to make a noise. That was the final straw. I didn't like living there anyway and now I felt unsafe. It was time to leave and find a different care home.

Chapter 19

Being disabled

The move to a care home in Hastings was the best move I have ever made. Before I moved, I had lost most of my confidence and my personality because, although the staff were really lovely, they were foreign so there were language barriers which made it very difficult for me. Sometimes I would have to spell words in lots of different ways. I stopped telling jokes as no one understood what I was trying to say. Some days I wouldn't speak to anyone. I felt lonely. I put on weight and would cry each time I saw my reflection. This went on for four years.

So even though I would have preferred my life to have been different this was the life that I was living. Things were not so bad. People said that I was inspirational. To be honest I disagreed. I was just living my life to the best of my ability. Even though I was disabled I was still determined to do the same as able-bodied people.

Whilst in Hastings I did a lot of activities. I went to the cinema loads of times. I went swimming. I had a barbecue on the beach. I went to birthday parties, christenings and funerals. I went clubbing and to pubs and restaurants. I did some charity walks and went to a farm and a zoo. I went to quite a few pub quizzes. I went to Glastonbury and on a day trip to London. Being in a wheelchair did not, and will not, stop me from doing anything. I learnt that with a mouthpiece I can paint. I designed a deckchair for the local council and won the competition and got the chance to have my design made into a deckchair.

One symptom of Locked-in Syndrome is uncontrollable laughing or a nervous laugh. I always smiled a lot before, but now I laugh when someone falls over. If someone tells a really bad and childish joke then I will find it funny. I find toilet humour really funny. I never found these simple things funny before my accident. Now I laugh if I burp. And I don't just giggle; these are proper, big, loud laughs.

I have a daughter who was only six years old when I went into hospital. She went to live with my sister and my six-year-old nephew. My daughter visited me a few times each week. They were my best and worst times. I missed her so much. I really missed the sound of her voice, and the warmth from her little arms when she gave me a hug was the best feeling in the world. I felt so jealous that someone else was caring for my little angel.

I was 27 years old when I fell ill. I do feel a little older but in most ways I feel about the same. I feel guilt and regret. I know that the stroke was not my fault but I do feel bad that my darling daughter was in the care system. She had foster parents. They did a great job. I'm just jealous that they had her and I didn't. I've had a recurring dream since my accident, where my daughter is in every dream and she is always a toddler.

When I was first diagnosed, I thought that I would be unable to do certain things. But with my stubbornness and my determination I'm doing so much better than I thought I would.

I've been disabled now for over ten years. I now accept that I am disabled. I spent years believing I wasn't like everyone else. I had to accept that I am disabled. I soon realised that people are staring at me because I'm disabled and not because of the way I look. I do find it rude when people stare. It's nicer if people just ask whoever is with me about me. Physically, in the first year I was at my worst. I never even thought that my health would improve.

At first, seeing my daughter once a fortnight was very hard. I would cry every week. I had supervised visits with her until she was sixteen. If she cried during a visit she was taken home without even a goodbye. So we never spoke about the serious stuff.

I have one sibling, a sister who is a year older than me. We have a love/hate relationship. Our personalities are very different. Even though we look alike neither of us is better than the other. I am an argumentative and confident person whereas she is quiet and sensible. She would back away from a fight whereas I would run towards it.

I found that things for disabled people are very slow and expensive. I had to wait for a year just to get a wheelchair! I watched a television programme where a character got Locked-in Syndrome. Within 24 hours he had no tubes and was moved into a home. I know that everyone is different but people should not believe that having a disability is that easy. It is not.

Also, if someone ends up in a wheelchair or with brain damage or paralysis in a TV programme, they always fully recover. It's lovely but sometimes life just isn't like that and being disabled isn't that bad. There are lots of good things about being disabled.

I spent just over five months in the hospital waiting for a care home to become available. Then in the last decade I've moved from one care home to another. I've always been the same. If I didn't enjoy my job I would get a new job. If I was unhappy with a boyfriend I would split up with him. Even now I would rather be single than with someone who does something which I cannot accept. I've always followed the saying, "If in doubt, get out".

In the Hastings care home

Chapter 20

My love life

When I was back in Hastings and I had my confidence back I began to date again. I didn't feel so ugly as I'd felt before. Lewis was my boyfriend before I met Justin. I'd first met Lewis in our local pub and we were together for about a year. He was never violent to me, unlike some people believed. He was always the type of man that you would not want to cross but if you are his friend he would do anything for you.

A friend was at a party and Lewis was at the same party. He was talking about me. Since my accident we had lost touch. My friend looked after me so she knew where I was. Lewis contacted my father who checked that I was OK to see my ex. I was fine and Lewis came to see me. I put my head on his muscly chest and he wrapped his strong arms around me. I couldn't believe my luck. Before the hug I thought I would never see him again. We had met over three years before and I still thought he was attractive and funny.

I'd never really thought about how a disabled person would have a romantic relationship. I remember having a conversation with an ex-boyfriend before I had the accident and we agreed that we would not have a relationship with a disabled person because we'd feel like we'd be taking advantage of them. Now I am a disabled person and my views are very different. I'm disgusted by my previous views. I think that people should be educated at school about different types of disabilities and illnesses.

I wasn't ready for the reactions from other people. First, we had to speak with my doctor and prove that I was not being taken advantage of. The management wanted us to mark on the calendar every time we had sex. The management wanted to know just in case the sex caused an infection. We never did that. We both thought that this rule was ridiculous and we never obeyed it. Surely I am old enough to know if I have an infection?

I wanted to feel normal but instead our relationship felt wrong and sordid. An agency carer actually asked Lewis what he was planning to do once he was bored with me!? I was totally offended. I felt like a dirty and old toy and not like the human being that I am. We were happy for about four months and then he had a major life change. I felt so useless. I just wanted to improve his life and I couldn't. It was nearly six months and I hadn't told my daughter that I was with Lewis. I knew that she would never accept Lewis because she hated him, so I had a difficult decision to make. If I stayed with Lewis, I would lose my daughter forever and she would make Lewis's life a nightmare. I loved them both. She is the only person in the whole world who can call me Mum and I couldn't watch Lewis fight for keeping in touch with his children. I didn't want to be without anyone but I had no choice. The last five months had been great but I wasn't ready for the comments from others and the rules made by the management. I felt like a small child doing something that I shouldn't have been doing. I believed that Lewis would prefer to be with a non-disabled girl. I thought that he would be better off without me. I made up some reasons and I wrote them down in a letter and gave it to him. We've stayed friends and I've said that in hindsight I should have just spoken to him. He read the letter and couldn't leave quickly enough.

Chapter 21

Getting stronger

At Hastings I started to make noises and they only got louder. I'm able to move my lips and form some words. I thought that if you hadn't spoken for years then you would never be able to talk. I went to see Professor Barbara Wilson again to see how much I had changed. She is a top neurological scientist and has written books on strokes. She assessed my condition. She showed me a short film about a woman that she knew. She has an illness which is very similar to mine. After 14 years she began talking. She is still improving, 22 years from her accident. I was told by lots of people that I would never make improvements but now I have partial Locked-in Syndrome instead of full Locked-in Syndrome which means that I am not as bad as the medical staff had originally diagnosed.

I've been at a care home in Eastbourne for about three years. I'm happiest here. I've accepted that I am disabled. I can see light at the end of the tunnel and I can now see a life after living in a residential care home. When I was told that I could never live independently in the community I was very upset. The thought of spending the rest of my life in a residential care home was awful. I spent about a year living on the second floor of the care home in Eastbourne. It was OK but the staff were always very busy because it was a nursing floor. I didn't need any help from the nurses at the time.

When I moved to the care home in Eastbourne, I started having all my food orally rather than as a liquid straight into my stomach. I didn't get any chest infections. I'd been told for years that if I took my food orally then I would be ill with chest infections. I was suffering from flatulence for years after my accident and I couldn't work out why. When I stopped having the liquid food my flatulence stopped. The liquid food is milk-based and I am dairy intolerant. No wonder I didn't feel fine.

I got moved to the ground floor, which is a rehabilitation floor. They don't have nursing staff on the ground floor and the staff encourage residents to be independent. I can drive my own wheelchair using a headrest. Before, I could only drive for an hour a week but when I moved downstairs I was able to leave my driving headrest on all the time so I could move about independently and go outside the building on my own.

I moved to the care home in Eastbourne thinking that it would just be a stepping stone to my own place. I was told that I could have intensive speech therapy. I was excited that I might be able to speak again. I've never been so aware that being able to communicate vocally is important. Some people are very impatient and some people still presume that if you cannot speak then you are unable to think. Just remember Stephen Hawking. He was extremely clever.

Attitudes towards people who cannot speak have improved over the last decade. People speak to me rather than just pretending that I am invisible. I sometimes just act vacant if I get treated as though I can't understand. I now use a lot of facial expressions. Most people understand what I am thinking without me having to say a word. There is a new technology which says what you are thinking. I am glad nobody can hear what I am thinking!

When I came to the care home in Eastbourne, I was doing speech therapy but after a few weeks this was cancelled. My funding got stopped for this because I was told that I would never speak again. I know that this is not true and that I will speak again. I know that I should try harder to talk. I will get back my confidence.

My neck got stronger. I was able to leave the premises without having a carer with me. I have what is called a Paddington tag on my chair with my name, address and contact number on. This helps to keep me safe. Now when I use the cycling machine in physiotherapy I actively cycle, which means that I have some power in my legs. In physiotherapy I can lay on my belly while I lift my head up. I attempt to drive my wheelchair around the area by myself but because I use my head to drive, I have to be in the correct position. A bump can stop me from being in the correct position and in Eastbourne a lot of the pavements have bumps in them.

Being disabled can be frustrating and some people talk to you as though you are stupid. I've never cared what people think about me and only occasionally do I let people's comments get to me. I guess I'm only human. You learn to be patient if you end up disabled. Unlike what you see on television it can take months or often years to get equipment that is needed.

Chapter 22

Changing

I've lived in four different residential homes. The homes are very different but also similar in many ways. Every home has staff on a night shift and staff on a day shift. Even though each shift is caring for the same residents there is always competition between the night and the day staff as to who is the best. Both are good at their jobs and nobody is better than the other. Yes, the night shift may seem easier than the day shift but during the day the patients are awake so the shifts are just different. In all homes the care staff seem to be under-appreciated by the management and there is a high turnover of staff. In all homes the communication between the staff is bad.

If anyone would like to be a carer then they should have a good sense of humour and have common sense. For example, if it's cold outside and you need a hat, scarf and gloves then common sense will tell you that the person you are taking out will also need a hat, scarf and gloves. They must have the ability to care without being too involved.

A good sense of humour is essential. Some people say laughter is the best medicine and I think they are right. After about a year I learnt how to smile again. I found things funny again. I began laughing at things which I never thought were funny before.

For over a decade now I have been living with Locked-in Syndrome. At first I hated it and I wanted to kill myself but I'm glad that I stayed alive. I was told that I would only live for two years but I don't give up. I don't know why but I found my health improving and I'm doing things that I never thought I'd be able to do.

I've changed so much. I can move my neck and some of my facial muscles. I'm not suctioned anymore and I don't need oxygen. I'm a lot more alert. My trick is not to listen to the specialists telling me that I am unable to do something. If you think that you can do something then try to do it. If you don't succeed then just try again at a later date.

So what do I want in the future? Having Locked-in Syndrome is not as bad as I thought. I'd love to be better but I know that I will never be the person I was before. I will improve, I just don't know to what extent. I don't want to live in a care home for the rest of my life but I know I will need someone to care for me.

I am so proud of my daughter. She has coped exceptionally well; better than most adults I know. I regret not living with my daughter through all those years. I still really miss her.

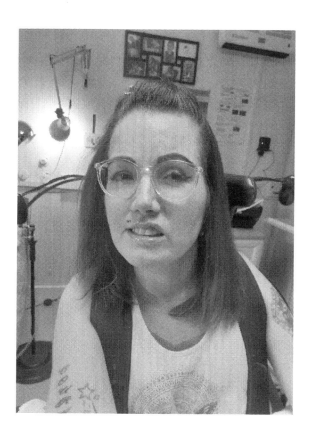

My Parents' Story

28th January 2008, 3.40 in the morning, our lives changed forever. We were woken by the phone, "It's the hospital, we have Tracey with us, she's very ill, can you come."

Our first thoughts were where is our granddaughter? Two hours later she is in school; our other daughter is going to look after her.

We arrive at the hospital. Tracey is in a coma looking as beautiful as ever, she just seems to be sleeping. Then you notice the spasms as her body tosses around fighting whatever is going on.

It's a drug overdose, the doctor says. It can't be, we answer, she had a bad fall in the gym, we say, landed on her head. That wouldn't cause it, they say. Three days later, in a neuro hospital, it's confirmed; a torn artery in the neck, a "very rare sports injury" they say, it has caused a massive clot in the base of the brain. Tracey is paralysed, this is her life now, she won't last three months we're told.

She is transferred back to our local hospital I.T.U. She's going to die, she'll never recover, can we let her go. We know Tracey would hate life like this so we agree, it breaks our hearts. Next day we're told she is young so we are going to keep her alive, she'll never get better but she a right to live, she'll only last 2 to 5 years anyway.

Not our Tracey, she fought back against all the odds, we sorted out a communication system looking up for yes and down for no, Tracey is scared, she doesn't want to die, she doesn't want to live like this. Five months later after being treated like she's stupid and doesn't know what's happening, she is transferred to a rehab unit. 280 mile round trip, what the hell? Soon she is back in hospital (pneumonia), altogether spending nine weeks of her time at the unit in hospital.

Here she has people calling her "it" and treating her as though she is stupid. Her care is diabolical, still she wants to die. Finally she is moved nearer to home, another nightmare begins, for Tracey as well as us, that's another story. In the meantime, we ride her lows and her highs with her, her fighting spirit keeps us going, she makes us laugh, she makes us cry but she's our Tracey, we love her and look out those who upset her.

Tracey has come a long way and we admire her determination to get or do what she wants out of life.

Love you Tracey x x x

Tracey aged 16

My friend's story

Tracey is an inspiration to all that know her. No matter what life throws her way she pulls through. I have known Tracey for more than ten years and consider her a close and valued friend.

I met Tracey through work and to say that she is outgoing is an understatement! When the rest of us were still half asleep at eight in the morning Tracey would be marching around the nursery with the children singing "The Grand Old Duke of York". All the parents and children loved her. Tracey was a valued member of staff and always worked to her full potential.

Outside of work Tracey is exactly the same, full of beans and always up for a laugh. I have such good memories of sitting in the pub, going out, having a dance and just having a night in at Tracey's old flat. We also went to salsa class where we were all put to shame. Tracey is the life and soul of any party and I'm sure many memories are to follow.

The news of Tracey's illness came as a shock to us all; it was only the previous night that we were all having a giggle at an Ann Summers party. Rumours start and I heard so many stories. Tracey's dad, who must have been going through such an ordeal, was brilliant and kept us posted on the real story. It didn't look good but I knew deep down that Trace would pull through.

I don't want to focus on the times of Tracey in the hospital; it was awful but must have been a million times worse for herself and her surrounding family who stayed so strong and supportive throughout, especially John.

Over time Tracey has become stronger and stronger, pulling through and adjusting to life in hospitals and homes, both good and bad. It was always hard leaving when Tracey was so far away; a few times we tried to smuggle her out.

It frustrated me to see people around her so clueless and patronising, talking to her as if she is stupid or can't hear. She is still the same person. I can't begin to think how that must feel.

The fact that Tracey can communicate is amazing. It can be slow at times but it's better than no communication at all. It's amazing seeing Tracey and her Dad, they are so quick. John has it mastered.

The truth is that Tracey may look different, she may not be as mobile as she was and she may not be able to speak but take all that away and she is still exactly the same. You can see the determination in her eyes, she won't give up. I feel so helpless at times, and powerless. When you see a friend in need you do everything in your power to help. I know even visits are appreciated but it just seems so little to offer.

Tracey was so independent, a free spirit who loved and cared for her daughter so much. To have that taken away must have been such a traumatic experience, a nightmare that you just can't be woken from. The worry of her daughter and that barrier being put up must have left such a helpless heartache. Tracey battled on when many people would have crumbled, and her daughter showed her Mum's fighting spirit. Looking at her now she is as beautiful and bubbly as her Mum, a little treasure.

I'm sure I speak on behalf of many who take life for granted, not just life's luxuries but the smaller things such as eating, having a bath or shower, getting dressed in the morning. Tracey needs someone to do all these things for her every single day. Once again Tracey continues without complaining. Maybe being put in this situation make you appreciate other things such as birds singing or a sunny day, maybe you notice things you have never noticed before. I'm sure Tracey sees people in a different light and knows who the important people are.

I'm so proud of Tracey and how far she has come. Every time I see her I can see how the determination has paid off. It must be a slow and painful journey but the end result is worth it.

Printed in Great Britain
by Amazon

46973651R00086